Alfred's Basic Piano Library

Duet Book • Level 2

TOP HITS!

P ★i a n★ o

Selected and Edited by E. L. Lancaster & Morton Manus

The pleasure young students get from adding popular music to their piano lessons has been well documented. The positive reaction we received from teachers following the introduction of Alfred's *Top Hits Solo Books* (Levels 1B–6) and *Top Hits Christmas Books* (Levels 1B–4) has been overwhelming. We are now pleased to add *Duet Books* (Levels 1B–4) to the *Top Hits* series.

Playing duets is important to the musical growth of the young pianist. Duets aid with the development of steady rhythm, listening for proper balance, and playing with appropriate dynamics. Finally, working together in a collaborative performance teaches more than just music. Not only does this duet series contain some of the most popular music ever written, but the arrangements are unique in a number of ways:

- The primo and secondo are equal in difficulty, with the melody distributed between both parts.

- Students are aided in achieving the correct balance between melody and accompaniment by dynamic signs and the inclusion of the lyrics with the melody only.

- For ease in reading, both the primo and secondo parts are written with the right hand in the treble clef and the left hand in the bass clef.

- Careful consideration has been given to spacing the music so that page turns are easy; measure numbers have been included for reference during practice sessions.

This book is correlated page-by-page with Lesson Book 2 of Alfred's Basic Piano Library; pieces should be assigned based on the instructions in the upper-right corner of each title page (the correlation for the Lesson Book of Complete Levels 2 & 3 is included in parentheses). You can even use *Top Hits Duet Book*, Level 2, with Alfred's Prep Course, Lesson Book E, beginning on page 7 and ending in Lesson Book F, page 33.

Since the melodies and rhythms of popular music do not always lend themselves to precise grading, you may find that these pieces are sometimes a little more difficult than the corresponding pages in the Lesson Book. The teacher's judgment is the most important factor in deciding when to begin each title.

When the books in the *Top Hits* series (Solo, Christmas, Duet) are assigned in conjunction with the Lesson Books, these appealing pieces reinforce new concepts as they are introduced. In addition, the motivation from the music increases student interest in piano study to successively higher levels.

Published by

HAL•LEONARD®
CORPORATION

ISBN 0-7390-0835-8

Distributed by

Alfred Music

Cover photos: Camera, popcorn box © 1999 PhotoDisc, Inc.
Backgrounds, movie clapboard © Eyewire, Inc.

T0016538

Do-Re-Mi

from THE SOUND OF MUSIC

Secondo

Use with Alfred's Basic Piano Library,
LESSON BOOK 2, after page 5
(or with LESSON BOOK
Complete Levels 2 & 3, after page 4).

Lyrics by Oscar Hammerstein II
Music by Richard Rodgers

Arr. by George Peter Tingley

Allegro

Play both hands one octave lower than written throughout.

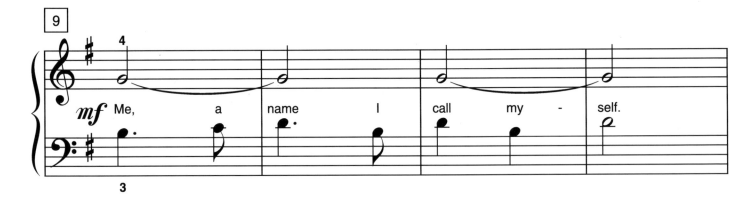

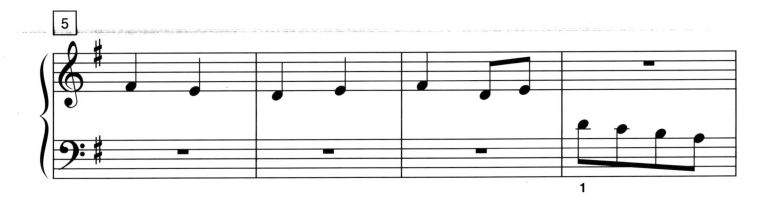

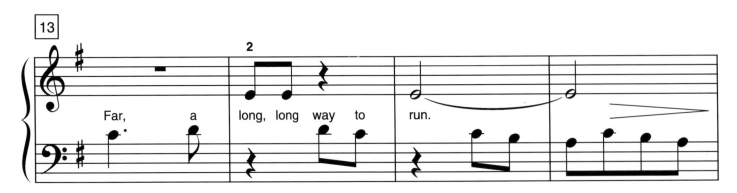

Do-Re-Mi

from THE SOUND OF MUSIC

Primo

Use with Alfred's Basic Piano Library,
LESSON BOOK 2, after page 5
(or with LESSON BOOK
Complete Levels 2 & 3, after page 4).

Lyrics by Oscar Hammerstein II
Music by Richard Rodgers

Arr. by George Peter Tingley

Allegro

Play both hands one octave higher than written throughout.

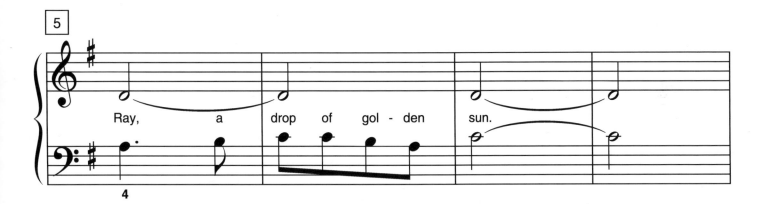

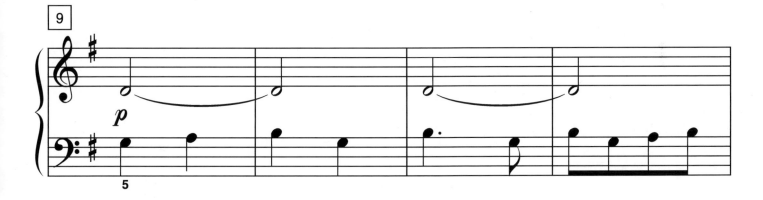

Do-Re-Mi
Secondo

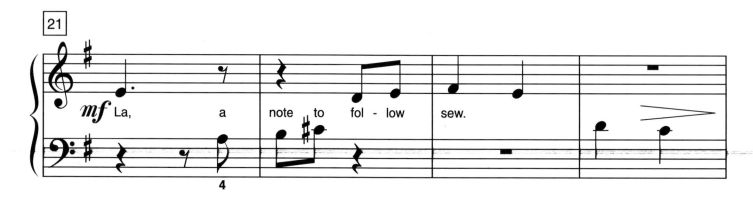

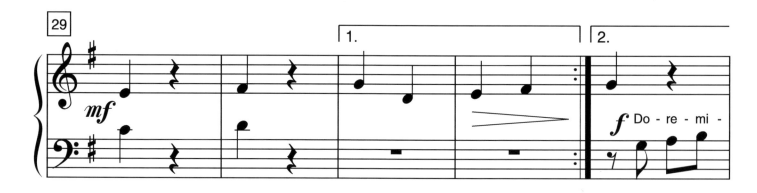

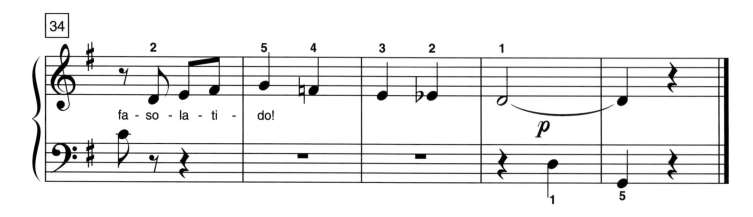

Do-Re-Mi
Primo

Use after page 11 (9).

Yellow Submarine

Secondo

Words and Music by
John Lennon and Paul McCartney

Arr. by Tom Gerou

Moderato*

Play both hands one octave lower than written throughout.

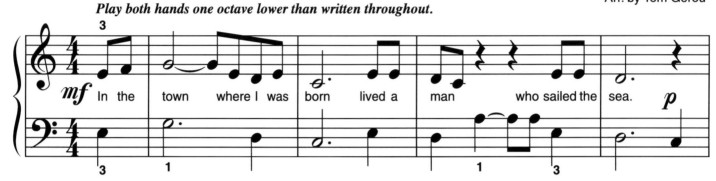

In the town where I was born lived a man who sailed the sea.

So we

sailed up to the sun

*Optional: Play eighth notes a bit unevenly,
in a "lilting" style: long short long short, *etc.*

Yellow Submarine

Primo

Words and Music by
John Lennon and Paul McCartney

Arr. by Tom Gerou

Moderato*
Play both hands one octave higher than written throughout.

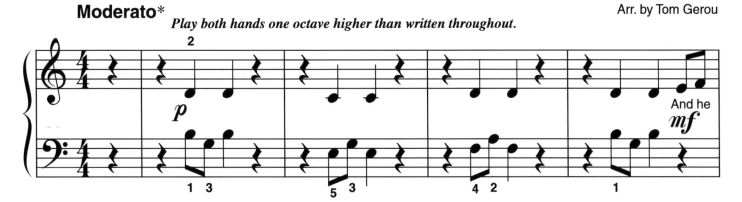

And he

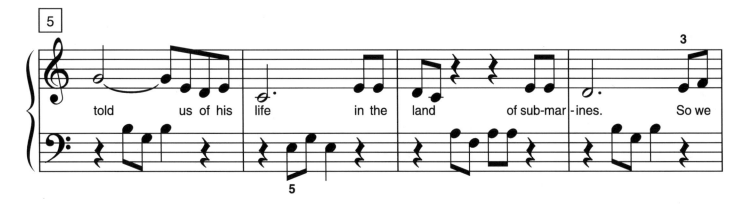

told us of his life in the land of sub-mar-ines. So we

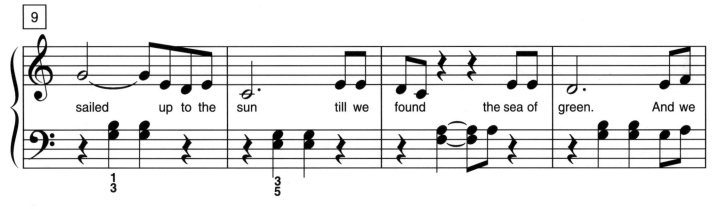

sailed up to the sun till we found the sea of green. And we

lived be-neath the waves in our Yel-low Sub-mar-ine.

*Optional: Play eighth notes a bit unevenly,
in a "lilting" style: long short long short, *etc.*

Yellow Submarine
Secondo

Yellow Submarine

Primo

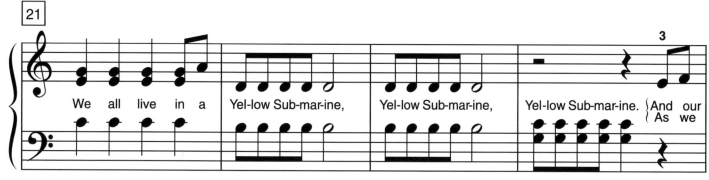

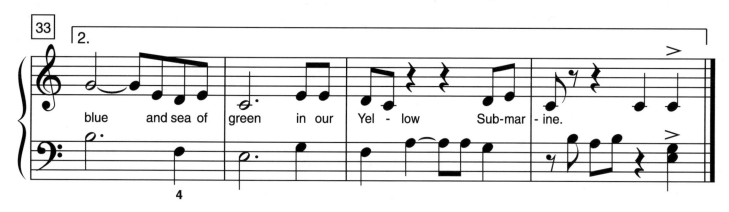

It's a Small World

from Disneyland and Walt Disney World's IT'S A SMALL WORLD

Use after page 19 (13).

Secondo

Words and Music by
Richard M. Sherman and Robert B. Sherman

Arr. by Margaret Goldston

Allegro

Play RH one octave lower than written throughout.

Use after page 19 (13).

It's a Small World

from Disneyland and Walt Disney World's IT'S A SMALL WORLD

Primo

Words and Music by
Richard M. Sherman and Robert B. Sherman

Arr. by Margaret Goldston

Allegro

Play both hands one octave higher than written throughout.

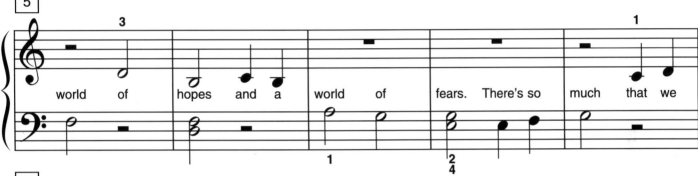

It's a Small World
Secondo

It's a Small World
Primo

Use after page 21 (15).

Colors of the Wind

from Walt Disney's POCAHONTAS

Secondo

Music by Alan Menken
Lyrics by Stephen Schwartz
Arr. by Sharon Aaronson

Moderato

Play both hands one octave lower than written throughout.

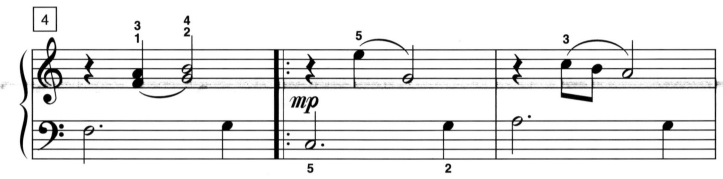

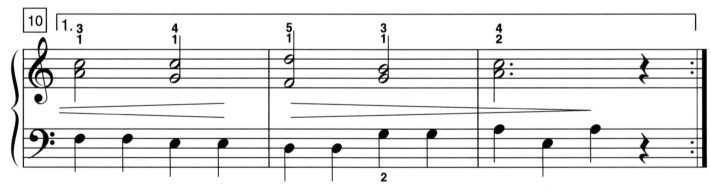

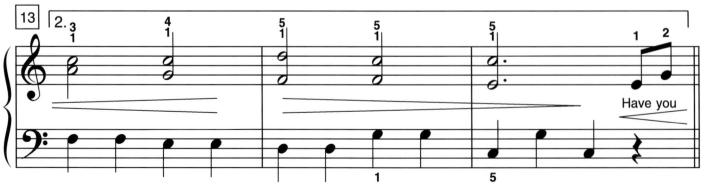

Have you

Colors of the Wind

from Walt Disney's POCAHONTAS

Primo

Music by Alan Menken
Lyrics by Stephen Schwartz

Arr. by Sharon Aaronson

Colors of the Wind

Secondo

Colors of the Wind

Primo

Use after page 25 (19).

You'll Be in My Heart (Pop Version)

from Walt Disney Pictures' TARZAN™

Secondo

Words and Music by Phil Collins

Arr. by Sharon Aaronson

Allegro moderato

Play both hands one octave lower than written throughout.

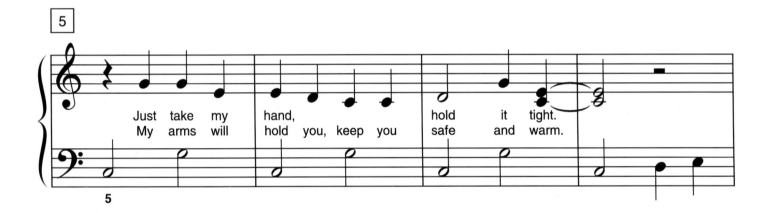

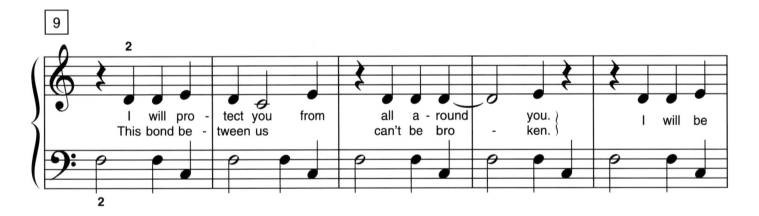

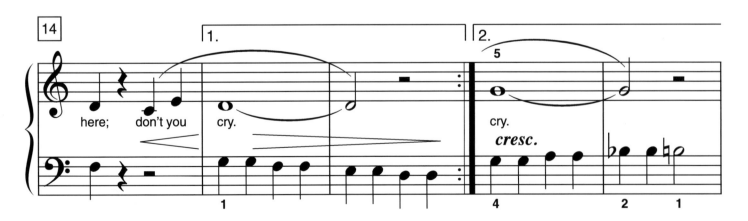

You'll Be in My Heart (Pop Version)

from Walt Disney Pictures' TARZAN™

Primo

Words and Music by Phil Collins

Arr. by Sharon Aaronson

Moderato

Play both hands one octave higher than written throughout.

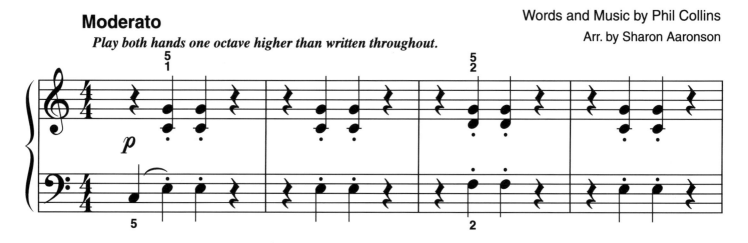

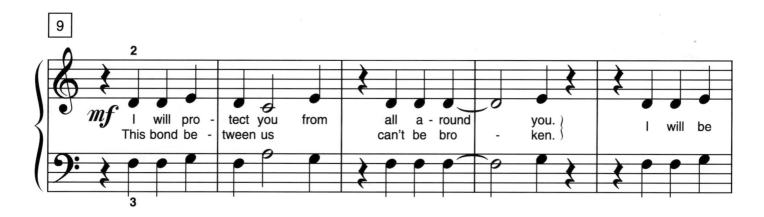

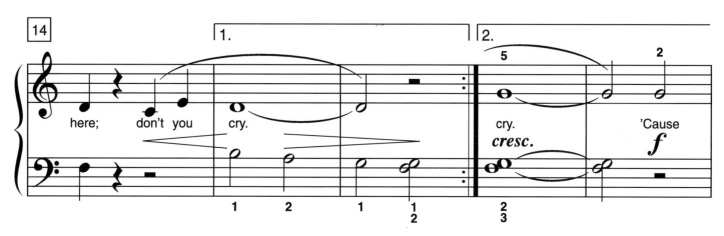

You'll Be in My Heart
Secondo

You'll Be in My Heart

Primo

My Heart Will Go On (Love Theme from 'Titanic')

from the Paramount and Twentieth Century Fox Motion Picture TITANIC

Secondo

Music by James Horner
Lyric by Will Jennings
Arr. by Dennis Alexander

Moderato

Play both hands one octave lower than written throughout.

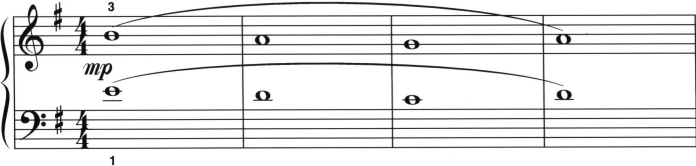

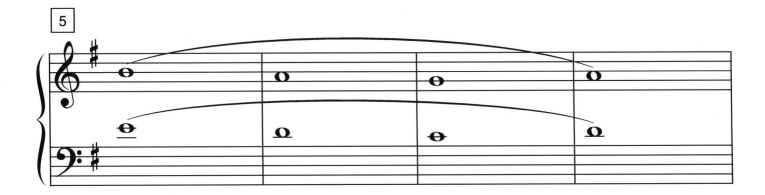

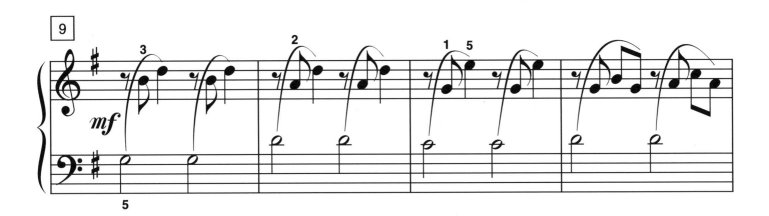

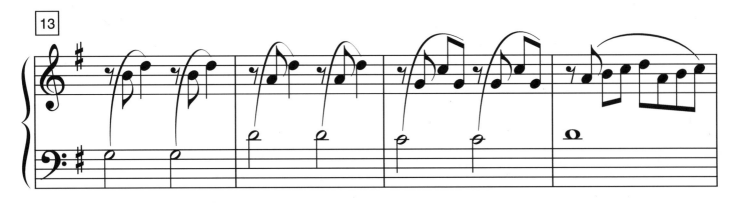

My Heart Will Go On (Love Theme from 'Titanic')

from the Paramount and Twentieth Century Fox Motion Picture TITANIC

Primo

Music by James Horner
Lyric by Will Jennings
Arr. by Dennis Alexander

Moderato
Play both hands one octave higher than written throughout.

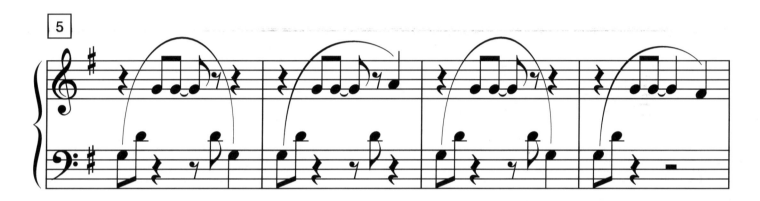

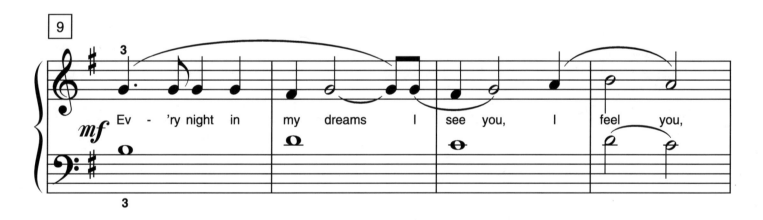

Ev - 'ry night in my dreams I see you, I feel you,

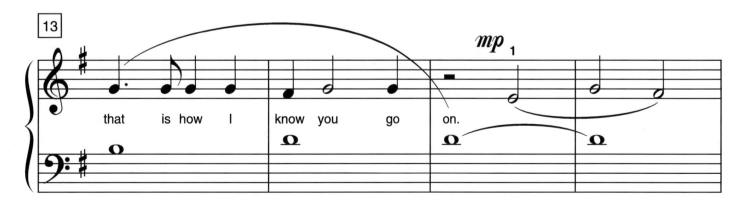

that is how I know you go on.

My Heart Will Go On
Secondo

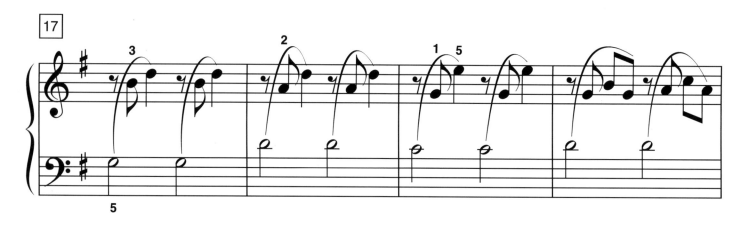

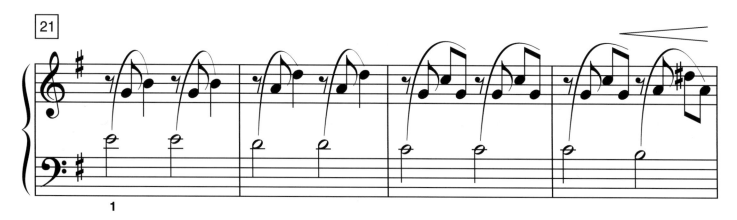

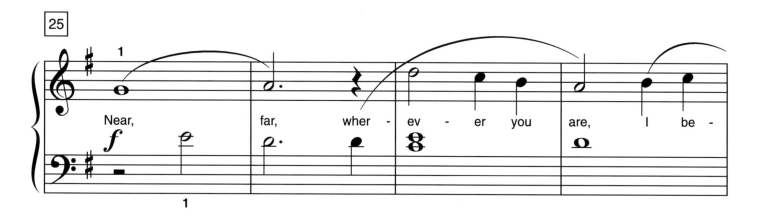

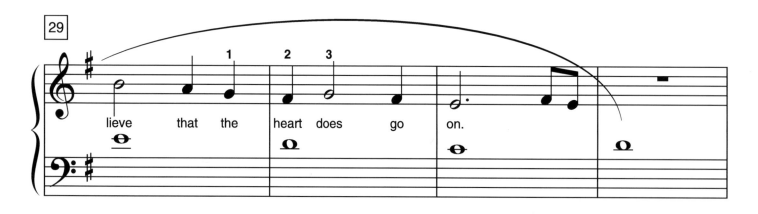

My Heart Will Go On
Primo

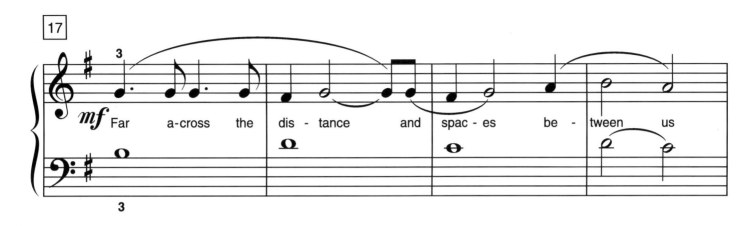

Far a-cross the dis - tance and spac - es be - tween us

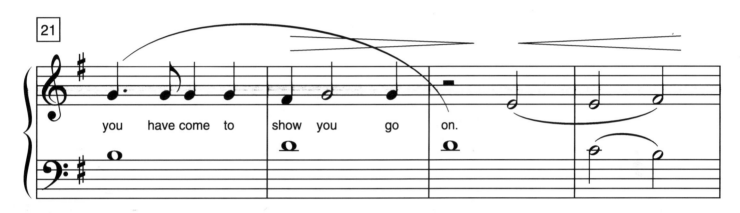

you have come to show you go on.

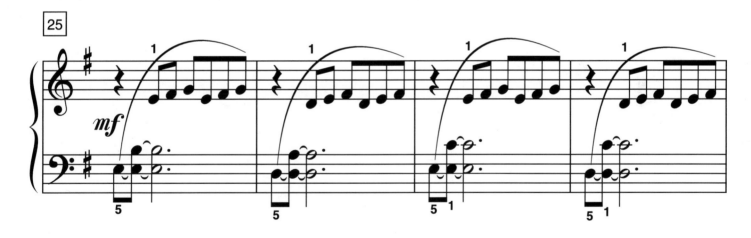

My Heart Will Go On

Secondo

My Heart Will Go On
Primo

Use after page 43 (37).

People in Your Neighborhood

from the Television Series SESAME STREET

Secondo

Moderato*

Play RH one octave lower than written throughout.

Words and Music by Jeff Moss

Arr. by Martha Mier

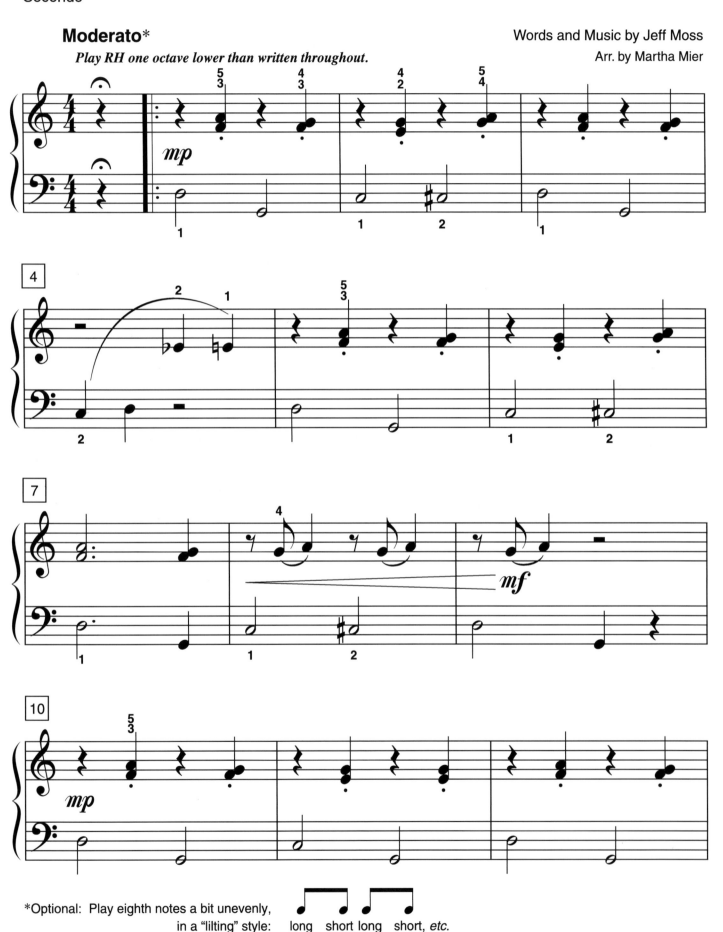

*Optional: Play eighth notes a bit unevenly,
in a "lilting" style: long short long short, *etc.*

People in Your Neighborhood

from the Television Series SESAME STREET

Primo

Moderato*

Play LH one octave higher than written throughout.

Words and Music by Jeff Moss

Arr. by Martha Mier

*Optional: Play eighth notes a bit unevenly,

in a "lilting" style: long short long short, *etc.*

People in Your Neighborhood
Secondo

People in Your Neighborhood

Primo

NEW!

Alfred's Basic Piano Library
TOP HITS!

**SOLO BOOKS
LEVELS 1B-4**

This new **Top Hits** series has been one that many teachers have been asking for—collections of graded popular music that correlate with *Alfred's Basic Piano Library*. We waited a long time to obtain just the right combination of hits from Broadway, Hollywood, television and recordings. The results are what you might expect from Alfred— great music arranged with care and creativity.

The arrangers selected for this series include Sharon Aaronson, Dennis Alexander, Christine H. Barden, Tom Gerou, Martha Mier and George Peter Tingley. These exciting new collections are certain to make practicing more fun for young students, and piano lessons more rewarding for music teachers!

Though **Top Hits** correlates with *Alfred's Basic Piano Library*, the arrangements are so perfectly graded, they may be used to advantage with any piano method.

Level 1B (16496)

Casper the Friendly Ghost
Do-Re-Mi
Edelweiss
I'm Late
I'm Popeye the Sailor Man
It's a Small World
Mickey Mouse March
My Heart Will Go On
    (Love Theme from 'Titanic')
Peter Cottontail
Puff the Magic Dragon
Rubber Duckie

Level 2 (16497)

The Bare Necessities
Beauty and the Beast
Be Our Guest
Can You Feel the Love Tonight
The Grouch Song
My Favorite Things
Part of Your World
The Rainbow Connection
Supercalifragilisticexpialidocious
Tomorrow
What a Wonderful World
Won't You Be My Neighbor?

Level 3 (16498)

Colors of the Wind
Cruella De Vil
Heart and Soul
I Just Can't Wait to Be King
Memory
My Heart Will Go On
    (Love Theme from 'Titanic')
Nadia's Theme
Rockin' Robin
The Sound of Music
The Unbirthday Song
A Whole New World

Level 4 (16499)

The Addams Family Theme
Axel F
Beauty and the Beast
Can You Feel the Love Tonight
Chim Chim Cher-ee
Don't Cry for Me Argentina
It's the Hard-Knock Life
Mission: Impossible Theme
Think of Me
Under the Sea
Yesterday

 **Available now from your favorite music dealer.**

Published by

HAL•LEONARD® CORPORATION

 **Distributed by Alfred Music**